Original title:
Healthy Love

Copyright © 2024 Book Fairy Publishing
All rights reserved.

Editor: Theodor Taimla
Author: Jessy Jänes
ISBN HARDBACK: 978-9916-756-80-5
ISBN PAPERBACK: 978-9916-756-81-2

Brimming Positivity

When dawn unveils its golden light,
A hopeful heart begins to sing.
Challenges melt in the morning bright,
As joy takes flight on a new wing.

With every breath, embrace the way,
Let laughter heal the deepest scars.
In every step, in every day,
Shine like the night's resilient stars.

Seek the beauty in the small,
Gratitude will softly grow.
Through rise and fall, hear the call,
Of life's ever-constant flow.

Peace in Togetherness

Underneath the azure sky,
Where fields of dreams together lie,
Hand in hand we wander free,
In unity, both you and me.

Whispers of the gentle breeze,
Carry love on sacred seas.
Together we shall find the way,
And greet the dawn of every day.

In moments shared, hearts align,
Creating bonds that intertwine.
Through trials faced, and joys held dear,
Our souls remain forever near.

Warm Fidelity

In the quiet of the night,
Where shadows dance in silver streams,
Love's warmth holds a steadfast light,
Embracing us in tender dreams.

Promises made in days of old,
Resonating through the years.
A bond of trust, pure and bold,
Shielding us from fleeting fears.

Through the seasons, hand in hand,
Silent vows we softly weave.
Together we shall firmly stand,
In the love we each believe.

Caring Reciprocity

Kindness flows like gentle rain,
Fostering a bloom within.
In the weave of joy and pain,
A sacred dance does soft begin.

Hands extended, intertwined,
Shared benevolence and grace.
In the mirror, love we find,
Reflecting in each other's face.

Acts of care and words so sweet,
We give and yet receive.
In the rhythm of hearts that beat,
We find the space to truly breathe.

Flourishing Together

In gardens where the sunlight gleams,
We wander through our shared dreams.
Leaves rustle with secrets old,
In our hands, the future we hold.

Unified in endless blooms,
Through shadows, our love assumes.
Rivers whisper tales of gold,
In hearts, our stories unfold.

Boundless Affection

Across the plains of endless time,
Our love remains a steady rhyme.
Stars above in silent night,
Glimmer with a pure delight.

Through the storms and fierce gale,
Our bonds tell a sacred tale.
Flowers blossom, seasons change,
But our affection stays the same.

Growth in Harmony

Roots entwined beneath the ground,
Growing stronger, weather-bound.
Through the seasons, thick and thin,
In unity, we both begin.

Every dawn and twilight's glow,
Together, side by side, we grow.
Nature's song, a sweet refrain,
In harmony, we break the chain.

Unwavering Bonds

Through life's unpredictable tide,
We stand together, side by side.
Challenges we face with grace,
In your eyes, I find my place.

Hand in hand, we face the sun,
In your heart, I find my home.
Unwavering in our shared quest,
Together, we are truly blessed.

Enchanted Commitment

In twilight's gentle, fleeting glow,
Hearts whisper tales only they know.
With every promise softly spoken,
An eternal bond, unbroken.

Infinite stars above do gleam,
Reflecting love's tender dream.
Hand in hand, spirits align,
A love enduring, ever divine.

Deeply Grounded

Roots entwine beneath the earth,
Nurturing love, giving it birth.
In moments still and ever sound,
Deeply, their spirits are bound.

Through changing seasons, steadfast stay,
Aligned in purpose, come what may.
Their hearts, a fortress never swayed,
In unity, their vows are laid.

Securely Attached

In love's cocoon, they find their place,
Each embrace, a tender grace.
With every touch, a story told,
Securely bound, two hearts of gold.

In whispered secrets, shadows cast,
Their love's imprint forever lasts.
Eternal comfort they have found,
Securely attached, heartbeats sound.

Uplifting Embrace

Beneath the sky, our spirits rise
Such hope within, no fear of ties
We find our dreams in daylight's glance
In every step, a fearless dance

Among the clouds, hearts intertwine
With endless love, we brightly shine
Strength in unity, we face the storm
In warm embrace, we keep hearts warm

In tender hues, joy lights our way
With open arms, we greet the day
Upon the breeze, our laughter sails
In every hug, a tale prevails

Sustained Euphoria

A spark ignites within the soul
Filling hearts with joy untold
In moments pure, we rise above
Sustained by warmth, a bond of love

Euphoria in endless streams
Illuminates our wildest dreams
We find the light in deepest night
Together soar, in pure delight

In joyous waves, our spirits play
Singing songs of love each day
From dawn to dusk, our hearts align
In happiness, our lives entwine

Genuine Harmony

In melodies of life, we blend
To notes of peace, our pathways bend
Each harmony, a sacred thread
With gentle touch, all sorrows shed

In every chord, sincerity
We find our place, eternally
With symphonies of heart's intent
In genuine love, we find content

Together in this dance of time
We craft a song, a rhythm's chime
In unity, our souls embrace
In harmony, we find our grace

In Sync with Grace

With every step, we find a place
Where hearts align, in sync with grace
The whispers of the wind embrace
A gentle dance, a tender trace

Our spirits glide on wings of light
Through shadows deep, we take our flight
In soft repose, we find our peace
In every joy, our souls release

Together on this path, we weave
With every breath, we rise, believe
In moments still, our lives entwine
In sync with grace, our hearts refine

Wholesome Hearts

In gardens green with morning light,
Where dreams and hopes ascend in flight,
Two hearts blend in harmony,
A love so pure, eternally.

Beneath the skies, a bond is born,
In whispered secrets, hearts adorn,
With hands entwined, they journey far,
Guided by their brightest star.

Through trials faced and joys embraced,
In every moment, love is traced,
A symphony of tender parts,
Resounds within their wholesome hearts.

Tender Care

With gentle touch and soothing voice,
In every moment, hearts rejoice,
Compassion flows, a healing stream,
In tender care, we find our dream.

In quiet nights, when shadows fall,
A tender heart responds to call,
With comfort found in loving arms,
We drift away from life's alarms.

Through trials faced and battles fought,
In every gesture, love is sought,
A beacon bright in darkest air,
Guided by this tender care.

Nurturing Soulmates

In the dance of life's embrace,
Soulmates find their sacred space,
With each step, they grow and heal,
In nurturing love, they feel.

Beneath the moon's celestial gaze,
Their boundless love begins to blaze,
Eternal flames in hearts so true,
In nurturing touch, they bloom anew.

Together facing highs and lows,
In union strong, their spirit shows,
Like rivers joining, seas unfold,
Their story of love, timelessly told.

Embrace of Trust

In shadows cast by doubt and fear,
The embrace of trust draws near,
With open hearts and open minds,
A sacred bond of trust it binds.

Through whispered words of honesty,
And actions pure, we clearly see,
The strength of trust, a guiding hand,
In every challenge we withstand.

With every promise kept and shared,
In moments tender, moments bared,
The embrace of trust, forever just,
In love's own wisdom, we entrust.

Blossoming Affection

In the garden where hearts intertwine,
Love's tender blossoms gently bloom.
Whispers of affection, pure and fine,
Paint joy's strokes in love's soft room.

Petals dance in morning's hue,
As hands entwine with gentle grace.
Affection blossoms, old yet new,
In the sacred, timeless space.

Through seasons warm and cold, they stay,
Nurtured by the sun and rain.
Affection's garden won't decay,
Love's touch heals every pain.

Each new bud a story told,
Of moments sweet and divine.
In the bonds that hearts hold,
Love's blossoms ever shine.

Unconditional Support

When the tides of trouble rise,
And darkness clouds your view,
Unseen wings lift you to the skies,
With love so pure and true.

In quiet whispers late at night,
Or hands that hold your heart,
Unyielding support, a guiding light,
No matter where you start.

Through the storms that life may bring,
Or dreams that you pursue,
Unconditional love takes wing,
Always standing true.

With every tear that's wiped away,
And obstacles they thwart,
In love's unending, warm display,
Behold this strong support.

Holistic Romance

Underneath the moon's soft glow,
Two souls meet in sacred dance.
In the realms where true loves grow,
They find their holistic romance.

Eyes that speak a thousand words,
Hearts connected, deeply bound.
In the silence, whispers heard,
Love's pure echo, perfect sound.

Together, in both joy and pain,
Their spirits blend, a single song.
Ever in an endless chain,
Bound where both hearts belong.

Eternal in their deep embrace,
Through time and space, they prance.
In love's caress, they fondly grace,
This beautiful, holistic romance.

Cherished Balance

In the dance where shadows meet,
And golden rays adorn the sky,
Life finds balance, pure and sweet,
Where love's true treasures lie.

Two hearts in perfect harmony,
A rhythm crafted by love's hand.
Balancing joy and agony,
On life's vast oceans and sands.

Cherishing each precious bit,
Of laughter, tears, and silent grace.
In balance, how their spirits fit,
In a warm, eternal embrace.

With every step, the balance stays,
Love's whisper guides them through the chance.
In their hearts and in their ways,
Exists a cherished balance.

Nurtured Souls

In the garden where dreams unfold,
Under skies of deepest blue,
Whispers of the wind, so bold,
Guide hearts loyal, kind, and true.

Sunrise paints the horizon bright,
With strokes of gold on morning dew,
Each moment, a gentle light,
Nurturing the souls like you.

River's song, a tender call,
Echoes in the quiet glade,
Through each rise and each fall,
Love's enduring serenade.

Peaceful Blossoms

In a meadow bathed in calm,
Where petals kiss the air,
Nature sings a tranquil psalm,
Beyond all worry, beyond all care.

Softly flows the silken breeze,
Over fields of emerald hue,
Whispering through ancient trees,
A peace that ever feels so true.

Daisies dance in gentle sun,
Tender blooms of every shade,
In their stillness, every one
Holds the peace of which they're made.

Harmonized Heartsong

Beneath the glow of twilight's grace,
Where shadows softly fade,
Two hearts find a timeless place,
In melodies they've played.

Voices blend in sweetest rhyme,
Lifting spirits high,
Every note a beat in time,
A song that must comply.

Hands entwined in bonds so strong,
In harmony they flow,
Dancing to a love-long song,
That only they could know.

Gentle Togetherness

In the hush of evening's rest,
Where moonlight softly beams,
Two souls find their peaceful nest,
In the realm of shared dreams.

Hands embrace in silent pledge,
Whispering without a word,
Boundaries met at the heart's edge,
Truth held and never blurred.

Time fades softly into night,
Stars blink in tender mirth,
Together they become the light,
That joins all things on earth.

Peaceful Partnering

In quiet corners, hearts align
Amidst the calm, our spirits twine
No storm shall break this bond we forge
For in each other, we'll find refuge

Hand in hand, our steps are light
Guided by love, through day and night
Beneath the stars, we softly tread
No words required, our hearts have said

A silent dance, a timeless song
In your embrace, where I belong
With every rhythm, we find our place
In peaceful partnering, we find grace

Together strong, yet gently free
The world around us, harmony
We're threads entwined in tapestry
Of love that spans eternity

Side by side, we'll face life's test
In union found, our souls find rest
Through every trial, love will sustain
In peaceful partnering, we remain

Nourished by Affection

Each tender glance, a seed is sown
In heart's rich soil, where love has grown
With every touch, our garden blooms
In fragrant peace, dispelling glooms

Your laughter's light, my soul's delight
Illuminates the darkest night
In every smile, a promise speaks
Of love enduring, through all peaks

Nourished by affection's grace
In your warmth, my safe embrace
Through seasons change, our roots are strong
Together we'll weather, where we belong

In whispered words, a sweet caress
Our love, a shield against distress
With every kiss, a vow is made
In warmth of heart, we'll never fade

Boundless is the love we share
In joy and sorrow, always there
Nourished by affection's glow
Together we will always grow

Gentle Waves of Us

Upon the shore where hearts collide
Gentle waves of us abide
With every crest, our love renews
In rhythmic dance, our souls fuse

The ocean's song, a lullaby
In every wave, a soft reply
To whispers carried by the breeze
In timeless sway, our hearts appease

Our love, a sea both calm and vast
A treasure trove in moments past
From dawn's first light to evening's hush
In gentle waves, our spirits blush

Together drifting, free yet bound
In each other's gaze, we're found
With every tide, our bond does grow
In gentle waves, we ebb and flow

Infinite the journey starts
Navigating by our hearts
Through every storm, we'll trust in us
In gentle waves, we find our trust

Harmonious Hearts

In sync with beats, our hearts unite
In perfect rhythm, day and night
A melody both soft and strong
In harmony, where we belong

Our souls, a song in flawless tune
Beneath the sun, beneath the moon
In every chord, our love aligns
A symphony without confines

Together, we compose our path
In joy and sorrow, tears and laugh
Through every note, our spirits blend
In love's sweet song, we find a friend

Our hearts, a concert grand and pure
In every verse, our lives endure
With every chorus, we proclaim
A love eternal, without shame

Harmonious hearts, entwined as one
In love's embrace, we've just begun
A timeless symphony of grace
In harmony, our perfect place

Bonded Bliss

In the shimmer of a smile,
A secret love is shared,
Together worth each endless mile,
Bonded hearts, prepared.

Laughter born of simple days,
Hand in hand, we find,
a thousand different loving ways,
To read each other's mind.

Whispers warm in moonlit night,
Serenade our dreams,
Glowing in each shared delight,
Flow like gentle streams.

Eyes that speak with no pretense,
Soulmates join as one,
In bounded bliss and sacred sense,
Eclipsing moon and sun.

On the path of life we tread,
In joys and trials, too,
The bonding bliss in words unsaid,
Shows love forever true.

Unified Growth

Roots that twine beneath the earth,
Branches climb the sky,
Unified in life's rebirth,
Together, reaching high.

Each leaf whispers shared belief,
In growing with the whole,
Unified from joy and grief,
We cultivate our soul.

Through seasons' endless, changing hues,
We hold our ground steadfast,
In struggles meet our truest dues,
Our bonds forever last.

Together we will rise and fall,
A symphony of fates,
Unified in nature's call,
Life's intricate landscapes.

Growth that shapes and deeply binds,
In unity expressed,
A journey where connection finds,
Its meaning manifest.

Golden Bonds

Threads of gold spun soft and bright,
Woven through the years,
Crafting bonds that feel just right,
In joyous cries and tears.

In sunlight's tender, golden kiss,
Moments softly gleam,
Golden bonds in timeless bliss,
An everlasting dream.

As days turn into decades past,
The golden threads remain,
In hearts and minds, forever vast,
Through pleasure and through pain.

Hand in hand, we face the sun,
In shadows and in light,
The golden bonds make us as one,
A tapestry so tight.

In the twilight of our days,
With stories spun gold-bright,
Our golden bonds, in countless ways,
Eternally unite.

Everlasting Bond

In twilight's soft and gentle gleam,
Two hearts unite, a perfect beam.
Unbroken threads, forever strong,
Together, they belong.

In every glance, a silent song,
A love that echoes loud and long.
Hand in hand, through days and nights,
Their spirit soars in flight.

With whispered words, and tender care,
A bond so pure, beyond compare.
Facing storms and sunny skies,
Love sees through every guise.

No distance breaks the ties they form,
In every breath, their hearts stay warm.
A dance of souls, forever graced,
In love's embrace, they're interlaced.

Eternal flames that never wane,
Against all odds, they'll rise again.
Everlasting bond so deep,
In their hearts, it will keep.

Tranquil Union

Beneath the stars, in midnight's glow,
Two souls converge, they ebb and flow.
A gentle hush, in tranquil space,
They find their sacred place.

In silken strands, their moments weave,
Each breath, a comfort they receive.
With every touch, the world stands still,
Their hearts, with love, are filled.

Whispered secrets, soft and clear,
Between them, there's no room for fear.
In silent trust, their spirits blend,
In peaceful joy, they transcend.

Through life's serene and quiet streams,
They sail together, sharing dreams.
In perfect sync, their hearts align,
In union, so divine.

Harmony in every chance,
They move as one in tender dance.
A tranquil union, ever so bright,
Guided by love's light.

Warmth Between Us

In every laugh, and every tear,
Your warmth is always near.
A comfort found in loving arms,
In your embrace, no harms.

With every smile, my heart's alight,
You are my day, you are my night.
Together, through the highs and lows,
A garden where love grows.

Soft whispers in the dark of night,
Your love, a beacon shining bright.
In every hug, and gentle kiss,
We find our endless bliss.

Through seasons change and years anew,
Our bond remains so ever true.
In warmth so pure, we find our place,
A safe and loving space.

The warmth between us, ever strong,
In cadence, our hearts belong.
Together, we will always be,
An endless symphony.

Flourishing Together

In morning's light and twilight's hue,
Together, we pursue the new.
Through growth and change, we find our way,
In love, we bloom each day.

With hands entwined, our roots run deep,
In unity, our dreams we keep.
The seeds we've sown in fertile ground,
In each other's love, are found.

Through trials faced, and storms we've braved,
In each other's eyes, we're saved.
With every step, and every stride,
Together, side by side.

In laughter shared, and tears that fell,
In our hearts, love's essence swells.
Flourishing with every touch,
Our bond, so potent, means so much.

In fields of green and skies of blue,
Together, we start anew.
With every breath and heartbeat's sigh,
Our love will never die.

Calm Hearts

In gardens where the lilies grow,
We find a peace we seldom know.
Beneath the sky, a silver arc,
Serene within the tranquil park.

Winds whisper through the ancient trees,
A melody that sets hearts at ease.
Gentle murmurs of the brook,
A soothing, natural poetry book.

In moments of this tranquil grace,
Worries vanish without a trace.
The world in harmony, aligned,
A sanctuary for the mind.

Time slows within these sacred spaces,
Emotion's ebb, no longer faceless.
Oh, calm within a heart sincere,
Contentment found, forever near.

Infinite Warmth

Beneath the sun's eternal rays,
Lies warmth that never fades away.
A kiss of light on every brow,
Infinite warmth, right here and now.

Golden hues stretch far and wide,
A vivid dream where hearts confide.
In every dawn, the promise shown,
Of love's eternal, radiant home.

Embraces shared beneath the stars,
Erase the hurt, erase the scars.
Bound by light, we stand as one,
In warmth, united, battles won.

In shadows, we no longer fight,
For warmth shines on, pure and bright.
A beacon in both night and day,
Guiding love along its way.

Quiet Resolutions

In the quiet of the morn,
New resolutions quietly born.
Whispers of a better path,
Lead us from the aftermath.

Promises made to the self,
Treasures found on wisdom's shelf.
No grandiose or loud affair,
Just inner peace beyond compare.

In silence, strength begins to grow,
A gentle stream starts to flow.
Transformations, subtle, pure,
Guide us toward a heart's allure.

Each small step and gentle care,
Crafts a life beyond compare.
In quiet, we find resolution,
A soul's serene, profound conclusion.

Sacred Trust

In silence, trust is softly born,
A sacred bond, both pure and warm.
Between our hearts, a bridge of gold,
A story of our spirits told.

Hand in hand, we walk this line,
Trusting love through space and time.
No fears arise, no shadows cast,
In sacred trust, we find our past.

Each word we speak, an oath so clear,
Building bonds that won't disappear.
In faith, we find a strong embrace,
A trust that time cannot erase.

Through storms of life and times of stress,
Our trust endures, no need to guess.
Sacred, solemn, understood,
A trust that makes our world feel good.

Peaceful Embrace

In twilight's gentle, fading hue,
We find where silence sings, it's true,
Beneath the sky's soft, velvet trace,
We rest in peaceful, warm embrace.

The stars above, their secrets share,
As moonlight dances in the air,
In whispered wind, our hearts link tight,
Two souls as one within the night.

Soft breezes carry dreams anew,
With every breath, our spirits flew,
To places where the heart can see,
In endless realms of you and me.

These moments, tender, full of grace,
No rush, no haste, just time to trace,
The paths we've wandered, side by side,
In life's sweet, peaceful, timeless tide.

In silence deep, our hearts still race,
In love's serene, untroubled space,
We find our world, our special place,
Held in night's calm, peaceful embrace.

Nurtured Companionship

In fields where golden blossoms grow,
We walk together, hearts to show,
The depth of bond that time can't sway,
In nurtured companionship, we stay.

Each step we take, with hand in hand,
We build a world of dreams so grand,
In every moment, joy we find,
With kindred spirits, souls aligned.

The path we tread is shared and true,
With trust and love as morning dew,
We face the days, in sun or rain,
Together, easing every strain.

For years may pass, and seasons shift,
But what we have, a precious gift,
Through eyes that speak, and hearts that know,
In nurtured love, we gently grow.

Forevermore, as time sweeps by,
Our bond remains, as clear as sky,
In every step, in life's grand show,
Our nurtured companionship will flow.

Affection's Haven

Within the heart's secluded realm,
A haven rests, where love does helm,
Soft whispers blend with tender gaze,
In affection's haven, hearts ablaze.

Where every glance, a thousand words,
In quiet hues, our voice be heard,
We find a peace, so pure, so bright,
In love's embrace, the gentle light.

Beneath the moon, in silver's sheen,
Together, crafting perfect scenes,
With every touch, the world is still,
In mutual trust, our hearts fulfill.

In moments shared, life's beauty lies,
Reflected in each other's eyes,
With every beat, and every sigh,
Affection's haven lifts us high.

This sacred space, where love does flow,
In boundless grace, we come to know,
In every day, and every night,
Our hearts, in haven, always right.

Golden Love

In threads of gold, our stories weave,
A tapestry where hearts believe,
In love that shines through day and night,
In golden hues, our souls unite.

The sun may set, the stars may rise,
But through it all, your love complies,
A constant glow, forever near,
In golden love, we conquer fear.

Each moment spent, a treasure found,
In love's embrace, our hearts are bound,
Through time's swift flight, and life's grand dance,
In golden love, a true romance.

With every dawn, a chance we see,
To grow, to love, to simply be,
In warmth that's felt, and softly shown,
In golden love, we've truly grown.

This golden love, our guiding light,
Through darkest days, and endless night,
Forever strong, forever true,
In golden love, I stay with you.

Calm within Connection

In moments silent, hearts entwine,
A tranquil breath, your hand in mine,
The world's a blur, we pause in time,
   A silent dance, our souls align.

Eyes meet eyes, no need for speech,
Understanding, just within reach,
A bond unspoken, gently fierce,
In calm, our hearts the silence pierce.

Whispered winds around us swirl,
Yet here we find our inner world,
In stillness deep, connection true,
A gentle peace, just me and you.

Embraced by night, stars softly gleam,
Together, we're a boundless dream,
In silence shared, pure hearts commune,
Within the calm, we both attune.

So hold this stillness, feel its grace,
In every touch and warm embrace,
In quiet moments, love's reflection,
We find our calm within connection.

Ever-Giving Affection

Your love, it blooms like morning dew,
In tender glances, ever new,
A gift that's endless, always true,
In every moment, I find you.

With gentle words and softest touch,
You show me love that means so much,
In every act, a heart so lush,
Overflowing, never hush.

Through every storm, in every weather,
You bring the sun, we shine together,
An ever-giving, boundless tether,
Our lives entwined, a love forever.

In laughter shared, in tears we dry,
Together, we both learn to fly,
An endless fount, so pure and high,
Your affection, our clear blue sky.

Forever grateful, this I swear,
For all your love, the ways you care,
A heart so open, always there,
Ever-giving, beyond compare.

Blossoming Commitment

In gardens where our love does grow,
A tender seed begins to show,
Nurtured by the sun's warm glow,
Our hearts together, ebb and flow.

Each promise whispered, roots take hold,
With every touch, the petals fold,
In quiet moonlight, tales retold,
Our bond, a flower, bright and bold.

Seasons change and time moves on,
Yet in our hearts, the same sweet song,
In every challenge, we grow strong,
Blossoming, our love lifelong.

Hand in hand, we face the light,
Together, hearts forever bright,
In every dawn and every night,
Our commitment, pure and right.

With every step, our love's secure,
A journey shared, so rich, so pure,
In blossoming, we find the cure,
For all life's trials, we're ensured.

Roots of Devotion

Beneath the soil, where secrets lie,
Our roots of love, they intertwine,
In depths unseen, they anchor high,
A foundation firm, forever shine.

Through storms and sun, they deeply reach,
A silent vow in every breach,
In every trial, a fervent teach,
Our roots of love, beyond the speech.

In whispers of the morning breeze,
In steadfast strength, they never freeze,
A bond so strong, with gentle ease,
Roots of devotion, hearts that please.

Through winters harsh and summers bright,
They hold us close, with all their might,
In love profound, we take our flight,
Bound by roots, our guiding light.

So here we stand, by roots upheld,
In every moment, stories meld,
In silent trust, our hearts compelled,
By roots of love, forever held.

Embrace of Trust

In a world of shadows, hearts align,
Trusting whispers gently bind.
Hand in hand, through night's embrace,
Love's whispers carve a sacred space.

Eyes meeting in a dance of grace,
Silent promises, hearts interlace.
In the realm where doubts dissolve,
Two souls in trust evolve.

Within the silence, echoes pure,
Soft caresses, intentions sure.
Through every trial, every gust,
Our hearts remain, in embrace of trust.

Flourishing Tenderness

In gardens where the soft winds play,
Tender blooms greet the day.
Petals open, hearts unfurl,
A gentle touch, a blooming pearl.

The sun's warm kiss, a lover's sigh,
Under a vast and azure sky.
In moments shared, in whispers hushed,
Tenderness blooms, hearts brushed.

Each leaf, a story, each flower, a song,
In nature's arms, where hearts belong.
Through seasons' dance, love's pure finesse,
Hearts entwined in flourishing tenderness.

Tranquility in Two

Beneath the moon's soft silver glow,
Two hearts find peace, in ebb and flow.
Silent whispers in the dark,
Echoes of love leave their mark.

In the stillness of the night,
Souls take flight in gentle light.
Hands entwined, hearts in view,
Together they find tranquility in two.

Stars above, in serene array,
Guide the lovers on their way.
With every breath, with every sigh,
Tranquility whispers, love stands nigh.

Embraced Serenity

In tender moments quiet and true,
Serenity's embrace feels ever new.
The gentle hum of hearts at peace,
Where love's whispers never cease.

A soft light bathes the tranquil scene,
Silent dreams where love has been.
Calm resides in every glance,
In life's simple, loving dance.

In serene meadows hearts do rest,
In each embrace, love's expressed.
In the stillness, ever free,
Dwells a lasting, embraced serenity.

Symbiotic Spirits

In forest deep where shadows play,
Beneath the dance of dappled light,
Two spirits weave the ancient way,
A bond formed in both day and night.

Their whispers blend with rustling leaves,
Their laughter echoes through the glen,
Symbiotic hearts our nature cleaves,
In unity, they live again.

A symphony of dusk and dawn,
Their paths converge in sacred trust,
Eternal footsteps linger on,
In every breeze, in sacred dust.

When moonlight bathes the sylvan glade,
Their forms entwine with silent grace,
Cosmic ties, forever made,
As love adorns this hallowed place.

Together bound in timeless trek,
Guardian spirits, side by side,
In dreams and whispers, they reflect,
Through boundless night, eternal guide.

In Tenderness We Trust

A gentle hand, a knowing glance,
In silence, truths are softly found,
With every breath, we take a chance,
In tenderness, our hearts are bound.

Through trials faced and tears we've shed,
Our spirits merge, two hearts as one,
In shadows cast and paths we've tread,
A love that blooms beneath the sun.

Each whispered word, a sacred vow,
Each heartbeat sings a timeless tune,
Together faced, the here and now,
In every loss, in every boon.

With every dawn, a fresh embrace,
With dusk, a promise soft as mist,
In tender trust, a sacred space,
In every touch, two souls have kissed.

Eternal flame, a guiding light,
Through all our days, through all our nights,
In tenderness we forge our might,
In resting hearts, our love delights.

Pure Devotion

In solemn gaze, two hearts align,
A vow, eternal and sincere,
In tender words, their souls entwine,
Pure devotion, love austere.

Through tempests fierce and calmest seas,
Their spirits soar, unwavering,
With gentle hands and bended knees,
In love's embrace, together cling.

A pledge within each fleeting glance,
A future carved from present trust,
In every step, in every dance,
Their bond withstands both time and dust.

Beneath the stars' eternal gleam,
Their hearts, a beacon shining bright,
In pure devotion, love supreme,
Guiding through both day and night.

And as the years entwine their path,
With wisdom, age, and boundless grace,
In pure devotion, they shall bath,
Till end of days, in love's embrace.

Vibrant Companionship

In fields where wildflowers bloom so bright,
Their laughter rings beneath the sky,
Through vibrant days and tranquil night,
Companions true, as years go by.

In shared adventures, hearts do dance,
Through every trial, every cheer,
A steadfast bond, a true romance,
Their every step, their love sincere.

In vibrant hues, their spirits blend,
A tapestry of joy and trust,
Each moment spent, a vivid end,
To all the loneliness and rust.

With every dawn, a fresh embrace,
With dusk, a promise free from fear,
In vibrant companionship, their grace,
In every realm, in every year.

Together face the boundless tide,
With hearts as one, with spirits freed,
In vibrant love, they shall reside,
With every care, with every need.

Robust Embrace

In the silence of the dawn, pure light breaks free,
Whispers of warmth in the golden sea.
Nature's arms, strong and wide,
Hold us close, with gentle pride.

The trees stand tall, their roots run deep,
Strength in harmony, a bond we keep.
Subtle whispers in the leaves,
Carry tales of ancient eves.

Mountains rise, steadfast and proud,
Touching heavens, defying every cloud.
Majestic, they stand, an eternal guide,
In their shadow, we never hide.

Waters flow, with a soothing grace,
Winding paths, in a robust embrace.
Unyielding tides, in their dance,
Offer life, in every glance.

In this realm, where strength appears,
Foundations of love, erase all fears.
Together we stand, hand in hand,
In the embrace of a resilient land.

Thriving in Unity

Beneath the sky, where dreams reside,
We find the strength, deep inside.
Together we thrive, hand in hand,
Building peace, across the land.

In unity, we find our way,
Connecting hearts, day by day.
Bound by love, we stand as one,
Underneath the shining sun.

With every step, our spirits soar,
United, we achieve much more.
In harmony, our voices rise,
Painting rainbows in the skies.

Trust the bond, in joyous blend,
Holding firm until the end.
Through every storm we navigate,
Together we shall celebrate.

Hand in hand, and heart to heart,
Our unity, a work of art.
In this bond, so pure and bright,
We journey towards the light.

Soulful Alliance

In the depths where shadows play,
A soulful bond lights the way.
Whispered secrets, shared in trust,
Forged in moments, pure and just.

Together we traverse, night and day,
Paths united, come what may.
With every heartbeat, close aligned,
Our souls in unity, intertwined.

Across the vistas, wide and grand,
We walk together, hand in hand.
Strengthened by each tender glance,
In this soulful, cherished dance.

Stars above, they softly gleam,
Reflecting every whispered dream.
In the silence, we find peace,
Soulful alliances never cease.

Hearts entwined, in sacred song,
Bonds that time cannot prolong.
In the embrace of night and day,
Our soulful alliance finds its way.

Undying Kindness

In a world where shadows roam,
Acts of kindness make a home.
Simple gestures, pure and bright,
Illuminate the darkest night.

With every smile, a seed is sown,
In hearts, a gentle love has grown.
Through fleeting time, and endless space,
Kindness finds its sacred place.

Hand in hand, with grace we tread,
A path where love is gently spread.
Through tears and laughter, joy and pain,
Undying kindness will remain.

No need for grandeur or display,
In quiet acts, it lights the way.
A touch, a word, a helping hand,
In kindness, we together stand.

Through the storms and sunny days,
Kindness guides us in its ways.
A beacon in the darkest night,
Undying, ever shining bright.

Blossoms of Serenity

In a garden quiet, dreams do weave,
Among the blossoms, hearts believe,
Soft petals whisper secrets dear,
Of peace and love that conquer fear.

Morning's light on dewdrops play,
Serenity begins the day,
In nature's arms, we find our rest,
With every bloom, we are blessed.

The breeze that dances through the air,
Lifts our spirits, light as prayer,
In the calm, our souls unfold,
A tapestry of pure, untold.

Among the flowers, moments freeze,
In their beauty, hearts find ease,
Blossoms teach us how to see,
The quiet paths to serenity.

Calm in Connection

In the stillness of the night,
Hearts connect with gentle might,
Whispers shared, no words required,
Peace ignites, as souls are inspired.

Eyes meet eyes, and silence speaks,
Calm embraces, spirit seeks,
In the bond of tender care,
We find solace, unaware.

Fingers touch, a simple grace,
Love unveiled in a gentle space,
In the quiet, pure and true,
Calm in connection, me and you.

Through the storms and through the rain,
Our hearts unite, dispelling pain,
In the bond we hold so tight,
Calm in connection, endless light.

Heartfelt Tranquility

In the hush of twilight's glow,
Heartfelt dreams begin to show,
Gentle whispers fill the air,
Of tranquil moments, pure and rare.

With each heartbeat, soft and slow,
Tranquility begins to grow,
In the silence, love's refrain,
Brings us peace, and stills the pain.

Through the night, a guiding star,
Leads us to where calm hearts are,
In the depth of quiet night,
Lies tranquility, pure light.

Heartfelt words, a soft embrace,
Create a sacred, peaceful place,
In the bond we come to see,
Heartfelt tranquility set free.

Secure Togetherness

Side by side, our spirits soar,
In togetherness, we find the shore,
In the bond of trust, we stand,
Secure together, hand in hand.

In the silence, dreams are spun,
Hearts united, two as one,
No fear can shake our solid ground,
Secure together, love profound.

Through the trials, through the tears,
We find strength, dispelling fears,
In the bond that's pure and true,
Secure together, me and you.

In the warmth of shared embrace,
We discover a sacred place,
Where love's light forever glows,
Secure together, heart knows.

Gentle Strength

In quiet whispers, strength does grow,
Veiled in calm, it softly shows.
Roots deep beneath the wildest storms,
A tender power, it transforms.

Mountains bow to patient might,
Rivers carve through stone in flight.
In stillness, find the force within,
A gentle heart, where dreams begin.

Enduring tides, a silent roar,
The shore is reshaped more and more.
Flex and yield, yet hold your form,
Through trials, gentle strength is born.

In twilight hues, the day unfolds,
A blend of warmth and whispers told.
Harness calm, let courage guide,
In gentle strength, let hope reside.

A steady hand through life's embrace,
In softness lies the truest grace.
The quiet ones, their strength revealed,
With gentle will, their fates are sealed.

Radiant Togetherness

Underneath the azure skies,
Where hearts unite and spirits rise.
In harmony, our voices blend,
In radiant togetherness, we mend.

Through laughter shared and tears that flow,
In unity, our strengths will grow.
A light that shines when we're as one,
Together, brighter than the sun.

Hand in hand, we face the night,
Together, we'll find endless light.
In every heart, a spark is found,
Together, lifted from the ground.

Across the fields of hope, we tread,
With love and dreams, our path is spread.
In every smile, in every glance,
Radiant togetherness, our chance.

As seasons change and days go by,
We'll hold each other, you and I.
In bonds of love, forever blessed,
Together, radiantly, we rest.

Embrace of Patience

In whispered moments, find your way,
With patience as your faithful stay.
Through winding paths, through trials deep,
An embrace of patience, secrets keep.

The river's flow, a lesson plain,
In patience, there is no disdain.
Each rock and bend, a story's trace,
To journey slow, with patient grace.

In waiting hands, the seedlings grow,
With time, their blossoms start to show.
A tender care, a watchful eye,
Patience lifts them to the sky.

In quietude, true wisdom lies,
The seldom seen, still often wise.
In every pause, an answer's found,
Patience brings the world around.

The stars above, they take their time,
Each twinkling light, a patient rhyme.
So hold your heart, with steady beat,
The embrace of patience is complete.

Eternal Tenderness

Beneath the moon's soft, silver gaze,
In quiet nights and endless days.
A love that whispers through the air,
Eternal tenderness, so rare.

The gentle touch, the tender kiss,
In moments pure, a timeless bliss.
Through every storm, through darkest night,
Eternal softness holds us tight.

In every breath, a heart's caress,
Within our souls, we do confess.
A love so deep, it knows no end,
In tender bonds, our hearts will mend.

With every dawn, a promise new,
In tenderness, our love we view.
A strength within, yet soft and kind,
Eternal tenderness, we find.

Through years that pass, through ages long,
In tender love, we both belong.
A gentle heart, forever true,
Eternal tenderness, with you.

Heartfelt Harmony

Beneath the skies we gently roam,
In twilight's soft embrace
When hearts beat loud, and call us home,
To love's eternal grace

With every step, a rhythm true,
Your breath a soothing song
The world's a canvas, bold and blue,
Where two souls can belong

In unity, we find our peace,
A dance that knows no end
Together, our joys only increase,
With every playful bend

No storm or shade can break our stride,
Our harmony stands strong
In love's embrace, we shall confide,
To you, I do belong

So here within this gentle sound,
We'll let our spirits fly
For in this love, we've truly found
Our heartfelt harmony

Tender Symbiosis

In whispers of the morning light,
Two hearts begin their day
A bond that's bound by sacred rite,
In ever-present sway

Your laughter, like a gentle breeze,
Inspires the flowers to bloom
Together, life is a masterpiece,
No trace of shadowed gloom

Each moment holds a tender grace,
A dance of give and take
In every glance, a warm embrace,
Our souls at peace, not fake

Joined by fate, our spirits meld,
In symbiotic trust
With hands entwined, our fears dispelled,
Our love a steadfast gust

From dawn to dusk, our journey flows,
Through every turn and thesis
For in your heart, I've come to know
A tender symbiosis

Trust's Tender Touch

In realms where shadows softly fall,
We find our steadfast light
With trust's tender touch, we stand tall,
Embodied in the night

Your eyes, a beacon through the dark,
Illuminate my way
With every step, our trust ignites a spark,
Turning night to day

Through winds of change and tides that turn,
We hold each other close
In trust's embrace, our souls will yearn,
For love that only grows

In silence, words are carried forth,
By gestures, kind and true
So trust becomes our compass north,
In all we say and do

Together, we are ever strong,
In trust's unyielding bind
For in your heart, I've found my song,
And peace is what we find

Balanced Togetherness

In the quiet of morning's dawn,
Our hearts find sweet repose
In balanced togetherness drawn,
A love that gently grows

Your smile, a beacon bright and warm,
Guides me through the day
In every storm, you are my norm,
The light along my way

We walk the path of life in stride,
Through valleys low and high
In every shadow, side by side,
Our spirits always fly

With every whisper, every glance,
A rhythm pure and true
In balanced steps, our souls advance,
To skies of boundless blue

Forever joined, our lives entwine,
In harmony's embrace
For in your love, I've come to find
A balanced, perfect space

Unified Tenderness

In the quiet glow of night,
Whispers soft as velvet breeze.
Two hearts bound within the light,
Unified, their tender ease.

Hands that meet in silent grace,
Eyes that speak of boundless skies.
A gentle touch, a warm embrace,
In their love, no room for lies.

Dreams that weave in endless streams,
Moments held in fond caress.
In this dance of shared dreams,
Unified in tenderness.

Footsteps sync on paths unknown,
Guided by their gentle art.
Two souls, their spirits grown,
Bound together, heart to heart.

Through the joys and through the fears,
Tender love is always near.
Unified, they wipe the tears,
In each other find their cheer.

Thriving Affection

Amidst the blooms of morning light,
Their hearts entwined in soft connection.
In shadows gone and future bright,
They bask in thriving affection.

Eyes that sparkle like the dew,
Voices mingling in delight.
Love that constantly renews,
Growing stronger with each night.

Through the storms and sunny days,
Their bond, unwavering and true.
In a thousand loving ways,
They find their home in me and you.

Hand in hand, they chase their dreams,
Building castles in the air.
With affection's endless streams,
They conquer all, their burdens share.

No distance wide, no time severe,
Can break their thriving, strong connection.
In every smile, in every tear,
They flourish in their pure affection.

Deeply Nurtured

Through time and tide, their love has grown,
Roots that reach the depths of earth.
In each word, affection shown,
Deeply nurtured since their birth.

Paths they walk with steadfast grace,
Nurtured by the hands that hold.
Love has found its sacred place,
In their hearts, a tale is told.

With patience as the seasons change,
Their bond grows deep in every hour.
No force can ever rearrange,
The deeply nurtured blooming flower.

Sharing sorrows, sharing joys,
Through life's wonders and its trials.
Their faith in love itself deploys,
Deeply nurtured, spreading smiles.

Echoes of their laughter ring,
In the valleys, on the sea.
Deeply nurtured, as they sing,
Love's sweet, timeless melody.

Fond Togetherness

In the stillness of the dawn,
Their hearts beat with gentle glee.
Fond togetherness is drawn,
In their eyes, love's constancy.

Steps in sync on sandy shores,
Whispers carried by the breeze.
Love in all its shapes and forms,
Fond together, hearts at ease.

Facing life and all it brings,
With a steadfast, loving grace.
Bound in fondness, their hearts sing,
Shining bright in every space.

Every sunrise, every night,
Fondness fuels their tender fire.
In each other's steadfast light,
They find all they could desire.

Through the years and endless days,
Love endures, a fond caress.
In their tender, joyous ways,
They build their fond togetherness.

Love's Gentle Hand

In twilight's gentle, calming glow,
Soft whispers in the evening's flow,
Hearts connect, a tender strand,
Guided by love's gentle hand.

Through storms and trials, firm they stand,
A bond unbroken, deeply planned,
With every touch, a sweet command,
All shaped by love's gentle hand.

Morning mist and dawning light,
Together facing darkest night,
Souls entwined, so brightly fanned,
Embraced by love's gentle hand.

Laughter shared, and tears so grand,
An endless dance on life's fine sand,
In every step, a joyful band,
Orchestrated by love's gentle hand.

In dreams where shadows softly land,
A tapestry of moments spanned,
We find our place in this grand land,
Forever held by love's gentle hand.

Unified Harmony

A symphony of hearts in tune,
Beneath the glowing silver moon,
Together they, in perfect rhyme,
Creating harmony, sublime.

Voices blend in twilight's air,
Uniting souls with tender care,
In every beat, a shared delight,
Their hearts beat on, a vibrant light.

In fields of blooming, fragrant hue,
Their spirits soar, a sky so blue,
Hand in hand through space and time,
Melodies of life, they climb.

Whispers of the gentle breeze,
Carry songs of joy and ease,
Unified in love's embrace,
An endless, boundless, sacred space.

Together strong, they face the dawn,
With every morn, a bonding drawn,
In the dance of life, renewed with grace,
Unified, they find their place.

Thriving Pair

Within the garden of their souls,
Two hearts entwined, a single goal,
To thrive together, hand in hand,
Life's wonders brightly spanned.

Each day a bud of hope in bloom,
Dispelling any trace of gloom,
With roots so deep and branches fair,
They flourish as a thriving pair.

Through seasons change, they cultivate,
A bond that time cannot abate,
Nurtured by the love they share,
Ever growing, a thriving pair.

The laughter shared, the dreams they weave,
In twilight's hush or morning's eve,
Together, face what life may dare,
Unyielding as a thriving pair.

In shadows cast, they seek the light,
Their spirits soar, a boundless flight,
Two hearts as one, beyond compare,
Forevermore, a thriving pair.

Heartfelt Flourishing

In the realm of hearts, they bloom,
Dispelling shadows, lifting gloom,
With every beat, a new delight,
Their love, an ever-shining light.

Hand in hand, they journey far,
Underneath the evening star,
Each step a testament to care,
Together in heartfelt flair.

In whispers soft, their secrets told,
A tapestry of life unfolds,
With every touch, their spirits lift,
In love, a never-ending gift.

They face the world with heads held high,
Beneath the endless, open sky,
In unity, their souls take flight,
Heartfelt flourishing, pure and bright.

With boundless faith in every day,
Through challenges, come what may,
Their love, a garden, richly fanned,
Together they will always stand.

Empowered Hearts

With strength unbound we rise, so bold
In unity, our stories told
A spark that lights the darkest night
Together, we embrace our might

Through struggles faced, our spirits soar
In every heart, an open door
No chains can bind what's forged in fire
Empowered hearts, we climb much higher

From ashes, embers start to glow
A force within begins to grow
Hand in hand, we walk the way
Towards a brighter, boundless day

Each challenge met, a battle won
The dawn of hope, a rising sun
With courage, love, we'll stand our ground
In empowered hearts, true strength is found

In every voice, a harmony
A testament to what we'll be
Resilient, fierce, and standing tall
Empowered hearts, we conquer all

Nature of Us.

Beneath the sky, our spirits blend
In nature's arms, our doubts transcend
The whispering leaves, a gentle song
In unity, we're never wrong

Through forest paths our feet will tread
With every step, we forge ahead
The river's flow, it guides our way
In nature's heart, we choose to stay

Mountains rise and touch the skies
With every peak, a new surprise
In valleys deep and oceans wide
The soul of nature, by our side

The sun and moon, in graceful dance
A timeless, ever-rhythmic trance
In every wave, in breeze so free
Nature molds our destiny

The stars above, a silent guide
In nature's course, our hearts confide
Beneath the moon, our spirits soar
In nature's truth, we find much more

Nurturing Hearts

Within the warmth of nurturing hearts
A bond of love so true, imparts
A gentle touch, a guiding light
Brings forth the day from darkest night

In every hug, a world reborn
In every tear, a lesson sworn
With tender hands, we build our dreams
Nurturing hearts, a radiant beam

Through trials faced, our love endures
With every challenge, strength ensures
In tender words and caring deeds
Nurturing hearts sow lasting seeds

Together, hearts entwine as one
In unity, our strength grows strong
With open arms and endless grace
We find our home, our sacred place

A whisper soft, a melody
The song of hearts in harmony
Nurturing love, we'll never part
For in each beat, a nurturing heart

Blossoms of Affection

In gardens where affection blooms
A fragrant path, dispels all glooms
With petal soft, and colors bright
In love's embrace, we find delight

Each flower tells a story sweet
In every glance, our hearts will meet
With every bud, a promise made
Of endless love, that will not fade

Through seasons change, our love remains
In gentle sun, and soothing rains
From roots so deep, to branches high
Affection grows, it will not die

In morning dew, and moonlit night
Our hearts align, the stars ignite
With tender care and loving touch
Affection blooms, it means so much

In every blossom, love inspires
With passion's flame, and heart's desires
A garden filled with pure connection
We dance among the blossoms of affection

Gentle Embrace

In the whispering breeze, hearts collide,
Soft as the twilight, where shadows reside.
Tender moments in the hush of night,
Wrapped in arms, everything feels right.

A caress so gentle, a love so pure,
In your embrace, I find my cure.
Eyes speak volumes in the muted hue,
Silent promises, found within you.

Moonlight waltzes on the quiet stream,
Love's soft murmur, like a serene dream.
Together we dance, slow and sure,
In the gentle embrace, our love endures.

Night's velvet curtain gently falls,
To the symphony of love, my heart calls.
In your arms, I rest my weary face,
Finding solace in each gentle embrace.

Serene Devotion

Under the canopy of endless skies,
Whispers of love in serene sighs.
Hands entwined, feeling complete,
In the quiet moments, our hearts meet.

Devotion deep in each tender gaze,
Through life's uncertain and winding maze.
Side by side, we face the storm,
In love's serene warmth, ever transforming.

Golden rays of dawn break the night,
In your arms, everything feels right.
Serene devotion, pure and true,
Guiding me in all that I do.

Every heartbeat echoes your name,
In silent devotion, forever the same.
Wrapped in your love, I find my place,
Serenity etched on your loving face.

Soulful Connection

In the depths of eyes, a soul revealed,
Connections forged, and bridges healed.
Heartbeat answers with rhythmic grace,
In every glance, I find my place.

Words unspoken, yet volumes told,
In the warmth of love, I unfold.
A soulful connection, pure and bright,
Guiding us through the darkest night.

Hearts intertwined in timeless dance,
In your presence, I find my chance.
A love so deep, it feels divine,
Your soul forever linked with mine.

Across the seas of time and space,
In your love, I find my place.
A soulful bond, ever strong,
In this connection, I belong.

Whispers of Care

In the hush of the twilight glow,
Words of care in whispers flow.
Gently tending to a heart that aches,
In your presence, each sorrow breaks.

Tender hands that hold and mend,
Lifting spirits, a faithful friend.
Whispers of care in the silent night,
Offering comfort till morning light.

No need for words in moments still,
Just being there, a heart to fill.
An embrace that speaks without noise,
In whispers of care, my heart rejoices.

Softly, like the morning dew,
Your care renews my spirit, true.
Through life's trials, always there,
In your whispers of gentle care.

Joyous Union

Beneath the skies so wide and blue,
Our hearts entwine, a love so true.
In laughter's dance, we find our way,
Together brightens every day.

Hand in hand, we greet the dawn,
A bond so strong, our love's new song.
The world may change, but we stay near,
A joyful union, hearts sincere.

From moments small to grand delight,
Our spirits soar, love takes flight.
Each whisper shared, each tender touch,
In joy, we know we've found so much.

With eyes that gleam, and smiles so bright,
We chase away the darkest night.
In love's embrace, we find our might,
Together making wrongs feel right.

In every heartbeat, every sigh,
Our souls unite, as time goes by.
A joyous union, strong and bright,
Forever bound, in love's soft light.

Enduring Serenity

In the whisper of the twilight breeze,
We find a calm, a gentle ease.
Our hearts aligned, in perfect sync,
In enduring serenity, we drink.

Through trials faced and hardships met,
No trace of doubt, no sense of threat.
With you, I find my every peace,
In this serenity, my worries cease.

Each moment cherished, time holds still,
Our shared silence, a soothing thrill.
With every glance and every smile,
Together strong, we journey miles.

In shadows cast by fading light,
We stand as one, with courage bright.
In love's embrace, we firmly stay,
Serenity guiding us each day.

Enduring like the ancient stars,
Our bond transcends the faintest scars.
In love's serene and lasting grace,
We find our ever-peaceful place.

Serenity in Partnership

In the morning's gentle rise,
We find love in each surprise.
Two souls bound with dreams so high,
In partnership, we touch the sky.

Through life's maze, hand in hand,
Together we both proudly stand.
Peace and calm our guiding light,
In every challenge, we unite.

Each footstep taken, side by side,
We navigate both deep and wide.
The waves may roar, the storm rage on,
But in our bond, serenity is drawn.

With whispered words and silent cheer,
We chase away each daunting fear.
In every shared and fleeting glance,
In partnership, our spirits dance.

Serenity draws us ever near,
In love's embrace, we persevere.
In partnership, we find our grace,
Together strong, in every place.

Mutual Nourishment

In the quiet of the night,
We nurture love, our guiding light.
Each touch, each word, a precious gift,
Mutual nourishment, hearts uplift.

Through trials faced and joys we share,
With tender care, beyond compare.
In each embrace, we find our strength,
Nourishing love at every length.

In laughter's echo, joy resounds,
Our bond grows deep with love unbound.
Together thriving, hand in hand,
Nourished souls, a timeless band.

With every breath, in harmony,
We grow as one, eternally.
In mutual care, we deeply thrive,
In love's rich soil, we come alive.

In mutual nourishment, we find,
A love so pure, a bond so kind.
Forever more, our hearts entwine,
Nourished souls, in love divine.

Gracious and Kind

In fields where the wildflowers grow,
Your heart shines, an endless glow,
With every gesture, sweet and mild,
You show the world a spirit, undefiled.

Through storm and calm, you stand tall,
Gracious and kind, you give your all,
With tender touch, and gentle eye,
You lift the soul, to feel the sky.

In whispers soft, your love does speak,
Healing the broken, the lost, the weak,
A beacon bright, in shadows cast,
Your kindness sails, a ship steadfast.

In gardens where the lilies spread,
Your grace leaves pathways we tread,
Each step, a dance, so pure, so light,
Gracious and kind, you warm the night.

O tender heart, O noble friend,
On you, all hopes and dreams depend,
With every dawn, your light we find,
Gracious and endlessly kind.

Eternal Bliss

In realms where stardust softly gleams,
Beyond the silver moonlit beams,
Lives a love, untouchable, pure,
An eternal bliss, divine and sure.

Through valleys deep and mountains high,
Our hearts will soar, with spirits nigh,
Bound in a bond, time can't dismiss,
Together, we find eternal bliss.

In whispers of the morning dew,
In each moment, I find you,
A symphony of joy, your kiss,
My one and only eternal bliss.

With every breath, a timeless creed,
In your embrace, my soul is freed,
Forever captured in your eyes,
Eternal bliss, our sweetest prize.

O gentle love, O boundless grace,
In you, my heart has found its place,
For in this dance, our souls unite,
Eternal bliss, our guiding light.

Gentle Souls

In twilight's calm and gentle breeze,
Where whispers of the day do ease,
Live hearts so tender, pure as gold,
These gentle souls, their stories told.

With every step, they softly tread,
On shores where dreams and hopes are fed,
Through acts of love, pure and serene,
They paint the world in colors keen.

Amidst the chaos, loud and wild,
Their presence soothes the weary child,
Like gentle streams that flow and wind,
These souls, with love, are always kind.

In silken threads, they weave a fate,
Of bonds eternal, love innate,
With gentle hands, they mend and mold,
The tapestry of life, unfolded.

O gentle souls, ever near,
With hearts so full, and spirits clear,
In you, the world finds peace and grace,
A haven in this vast, wild space.

Ever-Enchanted Affection

In gardens where the roses bloom,
And sunlight dances with the moon,
There lies a love, so pure, so true,
An ever-enchanted affection, just for you.

With each caress, with every glance,
We find ourselves in a timeless trance,
A love that whispers through the air,
Ever-enchanted, beyond compare.

In dreams where only lovers meet,
We share moments, tender, sweet,
A bond that time cannot unbind,
An affection ever-enchanted, intertwined.

With hearts that beat in perfect rhyme,
We walk through life, a dance in time,
Two souls as one, a perfect blend,
Ever-enchanted, without end.

O love, so deep, so boundless, bright,
In you, I've found my guiding light,
An ever-enchanted joy, divine,
From now until the end of time.

Harmonious Life

In the meadow, where dreams align,
Whispers of the wind, soft and kind,
Every blade of grass, a tune divine,
Nature's symphony, open your mind.

Sunrise kisses, the colors blend,
Mountains echo, the songs ascend,
Each heartbeat, a timeless friend,
In harmony, our spirits mend.

River's journey, through valleys deep,
Carrying secrets, memories keep,
A dance of life, as shadows steep,
In every ripple, the souls leap.

Starlit nights, where silence breathes,
Among the constellations, love weaves,
A celestial dance, as night concedes,
Life's holy rhythm, heart believes.

Echoes of dawn, a promise near,
Together in peace, without any fear,
Harmonious life, where dreams adhere,
The universe's song, always here.

Embracing Kindness

Glistening dew on morning's face,
Acts of kindness, endless grace,
In every heart, a sacred place,
Love's tender hands, warm embrace.

A smile given, a word of cheer,
Lighting paths, dispersing fear,
Golden threads, drawing near,
Kindness blossoms, crystal clear.

Hands that help, without a call,
Breaking through each icy wall,
In giving, we never fall,
Kindness lifts, embracing all.

Gentle whispers, to burdens ease,
Compassion flows, like the breeze,
In every touch, a soul appease,
Through kindness, the world finds peace.

In every beam of sunlight's glow,
Seeds of kindness, we shall sow,
In our hearts, let it grow,
A world of love, for all to know.

Serene Bonding

In the quiet shade, where shadows play,
Moments tender, hearts display,
Words unspoken, come what may,
In silence, love finds its way.

Eyes that meet, without a sound,
In each other's gaze, lost and found,
In gentle bonding, hearts are bound,
Serene love, so profound.

Whispers of dreams, shared in the night,
Candlelight souls, burning bright,
Together, soaring to new heights,
Serene bonding, pure delight.

Hands that touch, with soft caress,
In the quiet, love's confessed,
With you, every moment's blessed,
Serene bonding, heart at rest.

In the still, where hearts align,
Whispers of love, so divine,
Eternal whispers, timeless find,
Serene bonding, souls entwined.

Thriving Trust

In the firm ground, where roots ingrain,
Trust blooms, like summer's rain,
In every trial, joy and pain,
In trust, we thrive, hearts sustain.

Walking paths, hand in hand,
Faith unwavering, like the sand,
Together, strong we stand,
Trust, our fortress, grand.

In every promise, whispers true,
Through doubt and fear, we renew,
In trust, our love grew,
Thriving trust, between us two.

Eyes that believe, without a doubt,
In the silence, trust speaks out,
Through every storm, we devout,
Trusting hearts, brave and stout.

In the twilight, firm and just,
In each other, hearts adjust,
Together always, in thriving trust,
In trust, our love is just.

Milton Keynes UK
Ingram Content Group UK Ltd.
UKHW050754270624
444539UK00017B/29